Enrich B...
Grade

PROVIDES   Daily Enrichment Activities

HOUGHTON MIFFLIN HARCOURT

Printed in the U.S.A.

ISBN 978-0-547-58821-6

3 4 5 6 7 8 9 10 0982 20 19 18 17 16 15 14 13 12

4500360210   B C D E F G

Contents

CRITICAL AREA 1: Operations and Algebraic Thinking

Chapter 1: Addition Concepts

Chapter 2: Subtraction Concepts

Chapter 3: Addition Strategies

Chapter 4: Subtraction Strategies

Chapter 5: Addition and Subtraction Relationships

CRITICAL AREA 2: Number and Operations in Base Ten
Chapter 6: Count and Model Numbers

Chapter 7: Compare Numbers

Chapter 8: Two-Digit Addition and Subtraction

CRITICAL AREA 3: Measurement and Data

Chapter 9: Measurement

Chapter 10: Represent Data

CRITICAL AREA 4: Geometry

Chapter 11: Three-Dimensional Geometry

Chapter 12: Two-Dimensional Geometry

Draw to Add

COMMON CORE STANDARD CC.1.OA.1
Represent and solve problems involving
addition and subtraction.

1.

6 fish   and   2 more fish   __8__ fish

2.

4 cats   and   1 more cat   _____ cats

3.

4 dogs   and   3 more dogs   _____ dogs

 Writing and Reasoning Explain how your
drawing shows adding to in Exercise 3.

_____

_____

_____

Make Groups to Add

COMMON CORE STANDARD CC.1.OA.1
Represent and solve problems involving
addition and subtraction.

Choose two pictures.

Draw a line to show your choice.

Then write the sum.

1.		
2.		_____
3.		_____
4.		_____

Writing and Reasoning Change 3 to 5
in Exercise 4. How does that change your sum?

_____

_____

Match to Find the Sum

COMMON CORE STANDARD CC.1.OA.1
Represent and solve problems involving
addition and subtraction.

Match the addition story problems that have the same sum.

1. There are 2 black socks and 4 white socks. How many socks are there? _____	There are 2 small trees and 1 big tree. How many trees are there? _____
2. There is 1 big chair and 2 small chairs. How many chairs are there? _____	There are 5 black butterfiles and 2 white butterflies. How many butterflies are there? _____
3. There are 4 blue boats and 3 yellow boats. How many boats are there? _____	There are 3 white cats and 3 gray cats. How many cats are there? 6

 Writing and Reasoning Write a new addition story problem for one of the sums. Draw a picture to show the problem.

Complete the Bar Model

COMMON CORE STANDARD CC.1.OA.1
Represent and solve problems involving
addition and subtraction.

Complete the bar model. Write the addition sentence.

1. There are 6 birds in the nest.
   Then 3 more birds join them.
   How many birds are in the nest now?

   | 6 | ___ |

   ___

   _6_ ⊕ _3_ ⊜ _9_

2. Some sheep are in a pen.
   One more sheep joins them.
   Then there are 4 sheep. How
   many sheep were in the pen before?

   | ___ | 1 |

   ___

   _____ ◯ _____ ◯ _____

3. There are 2 flowers in a pot.
   Some more flowers are added
   to the pot. Then there are 6 flowers.
   How many flowers were added to the pot?

   | 2 | ___ |

   ___

   _____ ◯ _____ ◯ _____

Writing and Reasoning 2 more flowers
are put in the pot in Exercise 3. How many flowers
are there now? Explain.

_____

Where Does Zero Go?

COMMON CORE STANDARD CC.1.OA.3
Understand and apply properties of
operations and the relationship between
addition and subtraction.

Complete the addition sentence.
Use the picture as a clue.

1. $\underline{2} + \underline{0} = \underline{2}$

 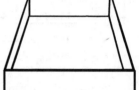

2.   ___ + ___ = ___

3.   ___ + ___ = ___

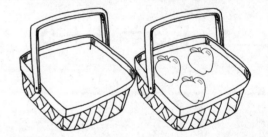

4.   ___ + ___ = ___

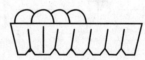 

 Writing and Reasoning What rule can you
make about adding with 0?

_____

_____

New Order, Same Sum

COMMON CORE STANDARD CC.1.OA.3
Understand and apply properties of
operations and the relationship between
addition and subtraction.

Write the missing number.

1.

$$1 + \underline{} = 3 + 1$$

2.

$$3 + 2 = \underline{} + 3$$

3.

$$2 + 4 = 4 + \underline{}$$

4.

$$\underline{} + 1 = 1 + 6$$

5.

$$\underline{} + 3 = 3 + 5$$

6.

$$7 + 2 = 2 + \underline{}$$

7.

$$2 + 5 = \underline{} + \underline{}$$

8.

$$\underline{} + \underline{} = 8 + 3$$

 Writing and Reasoning Look at your
answers. What rule can you make about the
order of addends in an addition sentence?

_____

_____

Complete the Sum

COMMON CORE STANDARD CC.1.OA.1
Represent and solve problems involving
addition and subtraction.

Draw more oranges to make 10.
Write the addition sentence.

1.

2.

3.

![Math Journal] **Writing and Reasoning** Make your own
problem like one above for a classmate to solve.

Stack the Story

COMMON CORE STANDARD CC.1.OA.6
Add and subtract within 20.

Read the story. Write the addition problem to solve.

1. Lea ate 4 🥨.
   Then she ate 1 more 🥨.
   Lea ate _____ 🥨.

2. Ron and José each ate 1 🍎.
   Tai ate 1 🍎, too.
   The boys ate _____ 🍎.

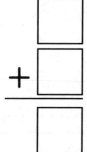

3. Miss Kim's class buys 4 🥛.
   Mr. Lin's class buys 6 🥛.
   Together they buy _____ 🥛.

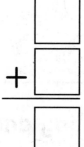

 Writing and Reasoning Create a story like the ones above. Have a classmate write an addition problem to solve it.

6-7-24

Draw to Find the Difference

COMMON CORE STANDARD CC.1.OA.1
Represent and solve problems involving
addition and subtraction.

Draw to show each story. Circle the part you are taking from. The cross it out. Write how many there are now.

1.

7 birds   5 birds fly away.   _____ birds now

2.

9 cows   6 cows walk away.   _____ cows now

 Writing and Reasoning Explain how you used your drawing to show Exercise 2.

_____

_____

_____

6-7-24

How Many Are There Now?

COMMON CORE STANDARD CC.1.OA.1
Represent and solve problems involving
addition and subtraction.

Solve. Complete the subtraction sentence.
Write the difference.

1. Phong had 3 boxes.

   He lost 1.

   How many does he
   have now?

   _____ – _____ = _____

   _____ boxes

2. There are 5 robins on a
   branch. 4 robins fly away.
   How many robins are
   there now?

   _____ – _____ = _____

   _____ robin

3. Miss Smith had 8 stamps.

   She lost 5.

   How many does she
   have now?

   _____ – _____ = _____

   _____ stamps

Writing and Reasoning Miss Smith lost 2 more
stamps. How many does she have now? Explain.

_____

_____

Name _____

6-7-24

Find the Missing Parts

COMMON CORE STANDARD CC.1.OA.1
Represent and solve problems involving
addition and subtraction.

Write a number to complete the problem.
Color counters to show the problem.
Write a subtraction sentence to solve.
Write how many.

1. There are 8 🌼 .   ◯◯◯◯◯◯◯◯

   _____ are short. The rest are tall.

   How many are tall?

   _____ 🌼 are tall.   ____ ◯ ____ ◯ ____

2. There are 9 🐰 .   ◯◯◯◯◯◯◯◯◯

   _____ are big. The rest are small.

   How many are small?

   _____ 🐰 are small.   ____ ◯ ____ ◯ ____

Writing and Reasoning Explain how to use ◯ to check your answer for Exercise 2.

_____

_____

_____

What's For Lunch?

COMMON CORE STANDARD CC.1.OA.1
Represent and solve problems involving
addition and subtraction.

Read the problem.
Complete the model and the number sentence.
Solve.

1. Allie has 10 grapes. She eats
   5 grapes. How many grapes
   does she still have?

   _____ grapes

   _____ − _____ = _____

2. Mr. Dobbs makes 8 sandwiches.
   He makes 1 peanut butter sandwich.
   The rest are cheese. How many
   cheese sandwiches does He make?

   _____ cheese sandwiches

   _____ − _____ = _____

Writing and Reasoning Write your own subtraction
problem. Use the bar model to solve your problem.

_____

_____

Solve the Story

COMMON CORE STANDARD CC.1.OA.8
Work with addition and subtraction equations.

Draw a picture to compare. Complete the subtraction sentence to solve.

1. Geo has 6 🍎.

   Lora has 2 fewer 🍎.

   How many 🍎 does
   Lora have?

   ____ – ____ = ____

   _____ has ____ 🍎.

---

2. Dana has 8 📖.

   Gabe has 1 📖.

   Tell who has more 📖.

   How many more 📖?

   ____ – ____ = ____

   _____ has ____ more 📖.

Writing and Reasoning Geo and Lora have
10 🍎. Dana and Gabe have 9 📖. Explain how to
compare 🍎 and 📖.

_____

_____

_____

Get Ready for School?

COMMON CORE STANDARD CC.1.OA.1
Represent and solve problems involving
addition and subtraction.

**Write numbers for the problem. Use the bar model
to solve. Write the number sentence.**

1. Jay has _____ pencils. Jay
has _____ more pencils than
Ken. How many pencils
does Ken have?

2. Sam has _____ scarves. Sam
has _____ more scarves than
Jane. How many scarves
does Jane have?

3. Lee has _____ books. Lee
has _____ more books than
Amy. How many books
does Amy have?

Writing and Reasoning How do you know which
number belongs in the top of the bar model in Exercise 3?

_____

_____

_____

A Zero Picture

COMMON CORE STANDARD CC.1.OA.8
Work with addition and subtraction equations.

Write the difference for each box. Use a black crayon to color in each box that has a zero difference to find a picture.

$8 - 0 =$ ___		$6 - 6 =$ ___		$6 - 0 =$ ___
$1 - 0 =$ ___	$5 - 5 =$ ___	$7 - 0 =$ ___	$2 - 2 =$ ___	$4 - 0 =$ ___
$2 - 0 =$ ___	$1 - 1 =$ ___	$3 - 0 =$ ___	$3 - 3 =$ ___	$5 - 0 =$ ___
$6 - 0 =$ ___	$7 - 7 =$ ___	$2 - 0 =$ ___	$8 - 8 =$ ___	$8 - 0 =$ ___
$3 - 0 =$ ___		$4 - 4 =$ ___		$1 - 0 =$ ___

Writing and Reasoning Write the difference for the following problem: $0 - 0 =$ ____. If you are right, your answer will match the picture above.

COMMON CORE STANDARD CC.1.OA.1
Represent and solve problems involving
addition and subtraction.

Take Apart Seven

Write the missing numbers to complete
the table to take apart 7.

1.	____ −	____	=	7
2.	____ −	1	=	____
3.	7 −	____	=	
4.	____ −	3	=	____
5.	7 −	____	=	____
6.	____ −	5	=	____
7.	7 −	____	=	____
8.	____ −	____	=	0

Writing and Reasoning What patterns do
you see in the table?

_____

_____

_____

Complete That Sentence

COMMON CORE STANDARD CC.1.OA.6
Add and subtract within 20.

Draw and write to show
a subtraction problem.

1.

2.

3.

Writing and Reasoning Draw your own picture. Have a friend write the subtraction problem that matches it.

Add in Any Order

COMMON CORE STANDARD CC.1.OA.3
Understand and apply properties of operations and the relationship between addition and subtraction.

Write the missing number.

1. $2 + 4 = \underline{\hphantom{4}} + 2$

2. $7 + 9 = \underline{\hphantom{xx}} + 7$

3. $6 + 7 = \underline{\hphantom{xx}} + 6$

4. $3 + 4 = 4 + \underline{\hphantom{xx}}$

5. $5 + \underline{\hphantom{xx}} = 5 + 5$

6. $4 + 6 = \underline{\hphantom{xx}} + 4$

7. $8 + 9 = \underline{\hphantom{xx}} + 8$

8. $\underline{\hphantom{xx}} + 2 = 2 + 9$

9. $6 + \underline{\hphantom{xx}} = 8 + 6$

10. $4 + \underline{\hphantom{xx}} = 8 + 4$

11. $2 + 5 = \underline{\hphantom{xx}} + 2$

12. $\underline{\hphantom{xx}} + 8 = 8 + 3$

Writing and Reasoning Look at Exercise 1.

How do you know that $2 + 4 = 4 + 2$? Explain.

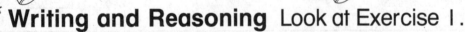

_____

_____

_____

Name _____

Count On Codes

COMMON CORE STANDARD CC.1.OA.5
Understand and subtract within 20.

| △ means count on 1. |
| □ means count on 2. |
| ☆ means count on 3. |

Follow the code to count on.

1. $2 \quad \triangle = \underline{3}$

2. $9 \quad \square = \underline{\hspace{1cm}}$

3. $4 \quad \square = \underline{\hspace{1cm}}$

4. $13 \quad \star = \underline{\hspace{1cm}}$

5. $10 \quad \star = \underline{\hspace{1cm}}$

6. $8 \quad \triangle = \underline{\hspace{1cm}}$

Write the starting number.

7. $\underline{\hspace{1cm}} \quad \star = 9$

8. $\underline{\hspace{1cm}} \quad \triangle = 4$

9. $\underline{\hspace{1cm}} \quad \square = 12$

10. $\underline{\hspace{1cm}} \quad \square = 9$

11. $\underline{\hspace{1cm}} \quad \star = 7$

12. $\underline{\hspace{1cm}} \quad \triangle = 11$

Writing and Reasoning Choose new codes for count on 1, 2, and 3. Write your own problems.

_____

_____

COMMON CORE STANDARD CC.1.OA.6
Add and subtract within 20.

No Doubles, No Problem

**Write a doubles fact for each sum if you can.
Mark an X on the addition sentence if you
cannot make a doubles fact.**

1. _1_ + _1_ = 2	**2.** ___ + ___ = 5 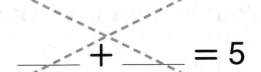
3. ___ + ___ = 10	**4.** ___ + ___ = 11
5. ___ + ___ = 9	**6.** ___ + ___ = 6
7. ___ + ___ = 4	**8.** ___ + ___ = 7
9. ___ + ___ = 13	**10.** ___ + ___ = 8

 Writing and Reasoning Draw ⬤ to show
why you cannot make a doubles fact for Exercise 2.

——

——

Domino Addition

COMMON CORE STANDARD CC.1.OA.6
Add and subtract within 20.

**Circle four dominoes. Write the addition
sentences for them.**

I. ☐ + ☐ = ☐	2. ☐ + ☐ = ☐
3. ☐ + ☐ = ☐	4. ☐ + ☐ = ☐

Writing and Reasoning Can you use
doubles to help you find any of the sums? Explain.

_____

_____

COMMON CORE STANDARD CC.1.OA.6
Add and subtract within 20.

Tic-Tac-Doubles

**Add. Circle doubles facts.
Draw an X on doubles plus
or minus one facts. Find
three in a row.**

1. $4 + 4 = \underline{8}$	**2.** $5 + 4 = \underline{\quad}$	**3.** $4 + 3 = \underline{\quad}$
4. $2 + 1 = \underline{\quad}$	**5.** $6 + 5 = \underline{\quad}$	**6.** $3 + 3 = \underline{\quad}$
7. $3 + 2 = \underline{\quad}$	**8.** $8 + 8 = \underline{\quad}$	**9.** $5 + 5 = \underline{\quad}$

Writing and Reasoning You want to make
three in a row in a different way. Which fact would you
change? How would you change it?

_____

_____

COMMON CORE STANDARD CC.1.OA.6
Add and subtract within 20.

Fact Balloons

Write an addition fact in each balloon.
Color doubles plus one or doubles
minus one facts blue.
Then color count on facts green.
Color doubles facts red.
Color other facts yellow.

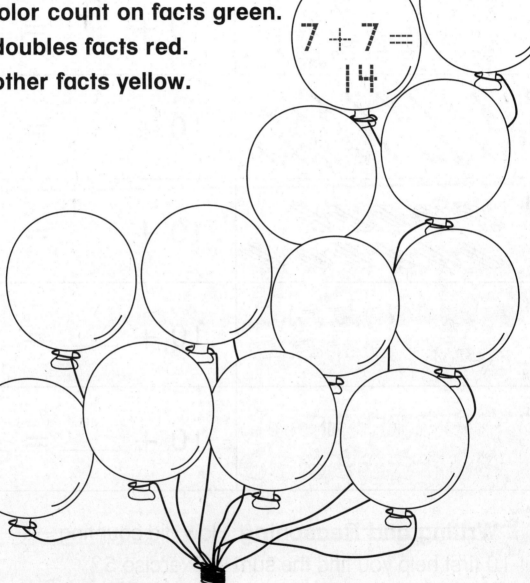

$$7 + 7 = 14$$

 Writing and Reasoning How did you decide
what fact to write in each balloon? Explain.

_____

_____

COMMON CORE STANDARD CC.1.OA.6
Add and subtract within 20.

Find Ten

Circle ten in each picture. Use the picture to complete the addition sentence.

1.	$10 + \underline{4} = \underline{14}$
2.	$10 + \underline{} = \underline{}$
3.	$10 + \underline{} = \underline{}$
4.	$10 + \underline{} = \underline{}$
5.	$10 + \underline{} = \underline{}$

Writing and Reasoning How did counting out 10 first help you find the sum in Exercise 5?

_____

_____

Make-a-Ten Match

COMMON CORE STANDARD CC.1.OA.6
Add and subtract within 20.

**Draw a line to match the addition.
Then match the sum.**

1.	$5 + 6$	$10 + 4$	12
2.	$8 + 6$	$10 + 3$	11
3.	$9 + 7$	$10 + 1$	16
4.	$7 + 6$	$10 + 2$	14
5.	$6 + 6$	$10 + 6$	13

 Writing and Reasoning Explain how you
matched the make-a-ten fact for Exercise 4.

_____

_____

Tens on the Table

COMMON CORE STANDARD CC.1.OA.6
Add and subtract within 20.

Complete the table. Write two different ways to make a ten. Find the sum.

1. $5 + 7$	__ + __ + __ 10	__ + __ + __ 10	
2. $7 + 6$	__ + __ + __ 10	__ + __ + __ 10	
3. $6 + 8$	__ + __ + __ 10	__ + __ + __ 10	
4. $7 + 8$	__ + __ + __ 10	__ + __ + __ 10	
5. $9 + 7$	__ + __ + __ 10	__ + __ + __ 10	

Writing and Reasoning What do you notice in the last column? Explain.

_____

_____

_____

Unlock the Sum

COMMON CORE STANDARD CC.1.OA.3
Understand and apply properties of
operations and the relationship between
addition and subtraction.

Draw a line to match. Find the sum.

1. $6 + 4 + 2 =$

$10 + 3 =$ _____

2. $3 + 6 + 4 =$

$1 + 8 =$ _____

3. $2 + 5 + 3 =$

$10 + 2 = \boxed{12}$

4. $1 + 6 + 2 =$

$8 + 3 =$ _____

5. $4 + 3 + 4 =$

$2 + 8 =$ _____

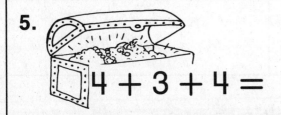 **Writing and Reasoning** Rewrite
$2 + 4 + 3$ in two different ways.

___ $+$ ___ $= 9$

___ $+$ ___ $= 9$

What Four?

COMMON CORE STANDARD CC.1.OA.3
Understand and apply properties of
operations and the relationship between
addition and subtraction.

Solve. Draw a picture.

1.	Lance sees 3 birds in the nest. Dustin sees 2 birds on a branch. Will sees 4 birds on the ground. Luisa sees 5 birds in the sky. How many birds do they see?	____ birds
2.	Juan eats 3 berries. Shayla eats 7 berries. Joseph eats 6 berries. Sara eats 3 berries. How many berries do they eat?	____ berries
3.	Four friends buy 17 books. Mateo buys 6 books. Lucy buys 4 books. Cara buys 2 books. How many books does Li buy?	____ books

Writing and Reasoning Explain how you added each number in Exercise 3.

_____

_____

_____

Use the Picture to Solve

COMMON CORE STANDARD CC.1.OA.2
Represent and solve problems involving
addition and subtraction.

**Write numbers in the problem to match the
picture. Complete the addition sentence to solve.**

1. There are ___**8**___ small fish
   in a pond.

   There are ___**3**___ big fish.

   How many fish are there?

   ___**8**___ + ___**3**___ = ___**11**___ fish

2. There are _____ black ducks
   by the pond.

   There are _____ white ducks.

   There are _____ gray ducks.

   How many ducks are there?

   _____ + _____ + _____ = _____

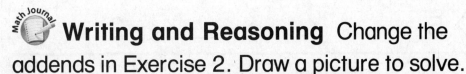 **Writing and Reasoning** Change the
addends in Exercise 2. Draw a picture to solve.
Write an addition sentence to check.

_____

_____

_____

Decode to Count Back

COMMON CORE STANDARD CC.1.OA.5
Add and subtract within 20.

| ◇ means count back 1. |
| △ means count back 2. |
| ☆ means count back 3. |

Follow the code to count back.

1.

10 △ __8__

2.

6 ◇ ____

3.

9 ☆ ____

4.

8 ◇ ____

5.

11 △ ____

6.

7 ☆ ____

Write the starting number.

7.

__6__ ◇ 5

8.

____ ☆ 2

9.

____ ◇ 4

10.

____ △ 6

Writing and Reasoning Using the codes above, write two problems.

Addition and Subtraction Riddles

COMMON CORE STANDARD CC.1.OA.4
Understand and apply properties of operations and the relationship between addition and subtraction.

Write the two number sentences described in the riddle. Then write the missing number to solve the riddle.

1. Add us together to make 9.
   Take one away from the
   other to get 3.
   What numbers are we?

   3 and ___6___

   3 ⊕ 6 ⊜ 9

   6 ⊖ 3 ⊜ 3

2. Our difference is 6.
   We have a sum of 14.
   What numbers are we?
   _____ and 10

   ___ ◯ ___ ◯ ___

   ___ ◯ ___ ◯ ___

3. Our difference is 2.
   We have a sum of 12.
   What numbers are we?
   _____ and 7

   ___ ◯ ___ ◯ ___

   ___ ◯ ___ ◯ ___

Writing and Reasoning Choose two numbers. Use them to write a riddle like the ones above. Write the two number sentences.

Fact Match

COMMON CORE STANDARD CC.1.OA.4
Understand and apply properties of
operations and the relationship between
addition and subtraction.

**Write the missing numbers. Use addition
to match the subtraction sentence.**

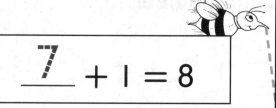

$\underline{7} + 1 = 8$

$8 - \underline{} = 4$

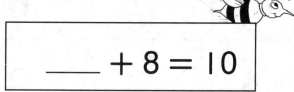

$\underline{} + 8 = 10$

$11 - \underline{} = 6$

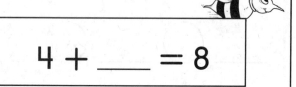

$4 + \underline{} = 8$

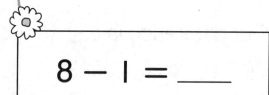

$8 - 1 = \underline{}$

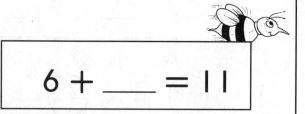

$6 + \underline{} = 11$

$10 - 8 = \underline{}$

 Writing and Reasoning Write an addition
fact and a subtraction fact for the picture.

____ ◯ ____ ◯ ____

____ ◯ ____ ◯ ____

COMMON CORE STANDARD CC.1.OA.6
Add and subtract within 20.

Write a Problem

**Write a problem for the number sentence.
Then make a ten to solve the problem.**

1. $17 - 8 = \underline{\quad?\quad}$

   Problem: _____

   _____

   _____

   Answer: _____

2. $15 - 6 = \underline{\quad?\quad}$

   Problem: _____

   _____

   _____

   Answer: _____

 Writing and Reasoning Explain how
you made a ten to solve the second problem.

_____

_____

Break-Apart Match

COMMON CORE STANDARD CC.1.OA.6
Add and subtract within 20.

Draw a line to match the subtraction.
Then match the difference.

I.	$12 - 5$	$13 - 3 = 10$ $10 - 2 = ?$	9
2.	$13 - 6$	$12 - 2 = 10$ $10 - 3 = ?$	8
3.	$13 - 5$	$12 - 2 = 10$ $10 - 5 = ?$	5
4.	$12 - 7$	$13 - 3 = 10$ $10 - 3 = ?$	7

 Writing and Reasoning Explain how you

matched the fact for Exercise 4.

_____

_____

Fill in Your Own Blanks

COMMON CORE STANDARD CC.1.OA.1
Represent and solve problems involving addition and subtraction.

**Write your own numbers in each problem.
Draw ◯ to solve.**

1. Labron has __8__ stickers.

   He gives some away.

   He has __5__ left.

   How many stickers does he give away? | __3__ stickers

2. There are _____ lizards on the tree.

   _____ more lizards join them.

   How many lizards are on the tree? | _____ lizards

3. Elena has _____ cookies.

   She gives some away.

   She has _____ left.

   How many cookies does she give away? | _____ cookies

Writing and Reasoning How did you solve Exercise 3? Explain how drawing a picture helps you find the answer.

_____

Missing Numbers

COMMON CORE STANDARD CC.1.OA.1
Represent and solve problems involving addition and subtraction.

**Choose a number to complete the story.
Solve. Use to help you.**

1. Macy has 8 markers. She loses

   __3__ markers. How many
   markers does she have left?

   $8 - \underline{3} = \underline{5}$

   __5__ markers

2. There are 15 balloons. _____ balloons are green. The rest are purple. How many balloons are purple?

   $15 - \underline{} = \underline{}$

   _____ purple balloons

3. Al has _____ books. He gives away 3 books. How many books does he have left?

   Butterflies

   $\underline{} - 3 = \underline{}$

   _____ books

4. There are 9 big fish. There are _____ small fish. How many more big fish are there than small fish?

   $9 - \underline{} = \underline{}$

   _____ more big fish

Writing and Reasoning What number of books can Al **not** have in Exercise 3? Explain.

_____

_____

Addition and Subtraction Facts

COMMON CORE STANDARD CC.1.OA.6
Add and subtract within 20.

Write a number sentence to match the picture. Then write a related fact.

1. ___ ◯ ___ ◯ ___

   ___ ◯ ___ ◯ ___

2. ___ ◯ ___ ◯ ___

   ___ ◯ ___ ◯ ___

3. ___ ◯ ___ ◯ ___

   ___ ◯ ___ ◯ ___

4. ___ ◯ ___ ◯ ___ ___

   ___ ◯ ___ ◯ ___ ___

 Writing and Reasoning Draw a picture. Color some objects one color and the rest a different color. Have a classmate write two number sentences for your picture.

Mice and Cheese Relate

COMMON CORE STANDARD CC.1.OA.6
Add and subtract within 20.

**Add and subtract. Draw a line from mouse
to cheese to match related facts.**

1. $7 + 2 = $ _____

$8 - 5 = $ _____

2. $3 + 4 = $ _____

$10 - 8 = $ _____

3. $3 + 5 = $ _____

$7 - 1 = $ _____

4. $2 + 8 = $ _____

$9 - 2 = $ _____

5. $6 + 1 = $ _____

$7 - 4 = $ _____

Writing and Reasoning Write a
third related fact for each pair above.

_____

_____

COMMON CORE STANDARD CC.1.OA.6
Add and subtract within 20.

Card Facts

Choose 3 numbers to make a subtraction fact. Write it.

Then add to check.

1.

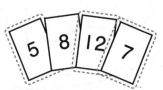

___ − ___ = ___

___ + ___ = ___

2.

___ − ___ = ___

___ + ___ = ___

3.

___ − ___ = ___

___ + ___ = ___

 Writing and Reasoning Change one number on the cards in Exercise 3 to make a new subtraction fact. Tell what you did.

_____

_____

Chicken and Egg Match

COMMON CORE STANDARD CC.1.OA.8
Work with addition and subtraction equations.

Write the missing numbers. Match each chicken to the egg with the related fact.

1.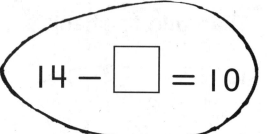

$\boxed{} + 2 = 7$

$14 - \boxed{} = 10$

2.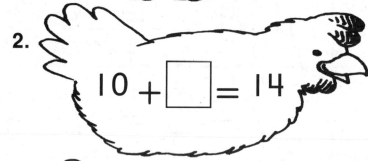

$10 + \boxed{} = 14$

$12 - 9 = \boxed{}$

3.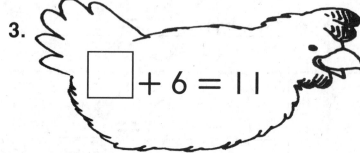

$\boxed{} + 6 = 11$

$7 - 2 = \boxed{}$

4.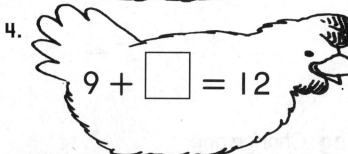

$9 + \boxed{} = 12$

$11 - \boxed{} = 6$

Writing and Reasoning Write a third related number sentence for each pair above.

Addition and Subtraction Riddles

COMMON CORE STANDARD CC.1.OA.8
Work with addition and subtraction
equations.

Write the missing number to solve the riddle.
Then write two related number sentences.

1. We have a sum of 6.
   We have a difference of 2.
   What numbers are we?

   4 and _____

   4 ◯ ___ ◯ 6

   ◯ ___ ◯ ___

2. We have a sum of 9.
   We have a difference of 3.
   What numbers are we?

   6 and _____

   6 ◯ ___ ◯ ___

   ◯ ___ ◯ ___

3. Together we make 12.
   Our difference is 0.
   What numbers are we?

   6 and _____

   ___ ◯ 6 ◯ 12

   ___ ◯ ___ ◯ ___

 Writing and Reasoning Choose two
numbers. Use them to write a riddle like Exercise 1.
Then write two related number sentences.

Coach's Choice

COMMON CORE STANDARD CC.1.OA.1
Represent and solve problems involving addition and subtraction.

Coach puts away some soccer balls.
Each bin holds 1 ball. There are 16 bins.

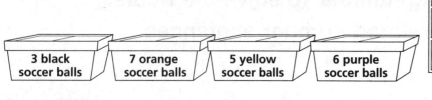

| 3 black soccer balls | 7 orange soccer balls | 5 yellow soccer balls | 6 purple soccer balls |

storage bins

Write addition and subtraction sentences to solve. Then circle yes or no.

1. Coach puts the black and the yellow soccer balls in the bins. Can she fit all of the orange soccer balls in the bins, too?

   yes   no

   ___ ◯ ___ ◯ ___
   black   yellow   total
   soccer balls soccer balls soccer balls

   ___ ◯ ___ ◯ ___
   bins   soccer balls bins left

2. Coach puts the orange soccer balls in the bins. Can she fit all of the yellow and the purple soccer balls in the bins, too?

   yes   no

   ___ ◯ ___ ◯ ___

   ___ ◯ ___ ◯ ___

Writing and Reasoning Coach empties 3 boxes and fills all the bins exactly. How can she do that?

_____

_____

Code Facts

COMMON CORE STANDARD CC.1.OA.6
Add and subtract within 20.

**List all the ways to make the numbers
using the code shapes shown here.**

1.

⬜

$$\underline{\hphantom{0}} + \underline{\hphantom{0}} = \boxed{}$$

$$\underline{\hphantom{0}} + \underline{\hphantom{0}} = \boxed{}$$

$$\underline{\hphantom{0}} + \underline{\hphantom{0}} = \boxed{}$$

$$\underline{\hphantom{0}} - \underline{\hphantom{0}} = \boxed{}$$

$$\underline{\hphantom{0}} - \underline{\hphantom{0}} = \boxed{}$$

$$\underline{\hphantom{0}} - \underline{\hphantom{0}} = \boxed{}$$

$$\underline{\hphantom{0}} - \underline{\hphantom{0}} = \boxed{}$$

2.

⬭

$$\underline{\hphantom{0}} + \underline{\hphantom{0}} = \bigcirc$$

$$\underline{\hphantom{0}} + \underline{\hphantom{0}} = \bigcirc$$

$$\underline{\hphantom{0}} + \underline{\hphantom{0}} = \bigcirc$$

$$\underline{\hphantom{0}} + \underline{\hphantom{0}} = \bigcirc$$

$$\underline{\hphantom{0}} + \underline{\hphantom{0}} = \bigcirc$$

$$\underline{\hphantom{0}} + \underline{\hphantom{0}} = \bigcirc$$

$$\underline{\hphantom{0}} + \underline{\hphantom{0}} = \bigcirc$$

Writing and Reasoning Choose another
number. Use the code to write all the ways to
make that number.

Shape Number Code

COMMON CORE STANDARD CC.1.OA.7
Work with addition and subtraction equations.

Draw the shape to make each number sentence true.

Shape Code

▲ stands for **8**   ● stands for **1**

■ stands for **4**   ♥ stands for **2**

1. $9 + 3 = \square + \square$ 2. $12 = \square + \square + \square$

3. $3 + \square = 7 - 0$ 4. $\square + \square = 5 + \square$

5. $16 = 6 + \square + \square$ 6. $7 + \square = 10 - \square$

 Writing and Reasoning Explain how you chose the shapes for Exercise 5.

_____

_____

_____

COMMON CORE STANDARD CC.1.OA.6
Add and subtract within 20.

Math Fact Hints

Use the hint to add or subtract.

1. Hint: One addend is 1 less than the other.

$$\boxed{} + \boxed{} = \boxed{11}$$

2. Hint: The difference is 10.

$$\boxed{15} - \boxed{} = \boxed{}$$

3. Hint: Use the number 9 two times in this math fact.

$$\boxed{} - \boxed{} = \boxed{9}$$

4. Hint: One addend is 3 more than the other.

$$\boxed{} + \boxed{} = \boxed{13}$$

5. Hint: The difference is greater than 6 and less than 8.

$$\boxed{9} - \boxed{} = \boxed{}$$

6. Hint: The addends are the same.

$$\boxed{} + \boxed{} = \boxed{}$$

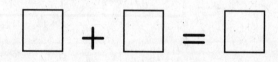 **Writing and Reasoning** What other fact can you write for Exercise 6? Explain.

_____

COMMON CORE STANDARD CC.1.NBT.1
Extend the counting sequence.

What Is Missing?

Write the missing numbers
in the Counting Chart.

1	2	3	4	5	6	7	8	9	10
	12	13	14	15	16	17	18	19	20
21			24	25	26			29	30
31	32	33		35		37	38		40
	43	44		46	47	48			50
	52	53	54	55	56	57			60
61			64	65	66	67		69	70
71	72		74	75	76			79	80
81	82	83		85		87	88	89	90
91	92	93	94		96	97	98	99	
	102	103	104	105	106	107	108	109	110
111	112	113	114			117	118	119	

Writing and Reasoning How did you know the
number to write after 119?

_____

_____

COMMON CORE STANDARD CC.1.NBT.1
Extend the counting sequence.

Bee Counts

Which flowers do the bees visit? Count forward by tens. Draw lines to show the path from each bee to its hive.

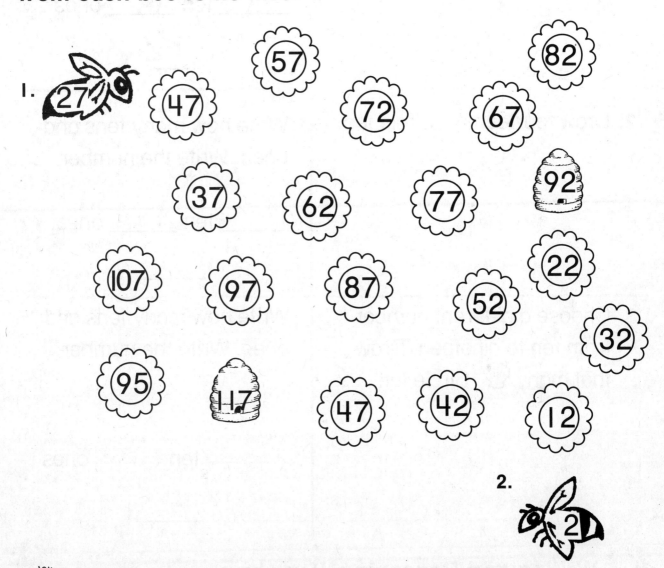

Writing and Reasoning If your starting number was 23 instead of 27 in Exercise 1, what do you think your ending number would be? Explain.

_____

_____

Name _____

Draw Ten and Some More

COMMON CORE STANDARD CC.1.NBT.2b
Understand place value.

1. Draw twelve 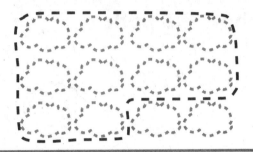. Circle ten.

Write how many tens and ones. Write the number.

_____1_____ ten _____2_____ ones

_____12_____

---

2. Draw fourteen 🪏. Circle ten.

Write how many tens and ones. Write the number.

_____ ten _____ ones

_____

---

3. Choose a different number from ten to nineteen. Draw that many 🐚. Circle ten.

Write how many tens and ones. Write the number.

_____ ten _____ ones

_____

Writing and Reasoning If you have thirteen starfish and you give ten away, how many will you have left? Draw to show your work. Write the numbers.

_____ tens _____ ones = _____ starfish

Name _____

Lesson 6.4
Enrich

COMMON CORE STANDARD CC.1.NBT.2b
Understand place value.

Turtle Match, Turtle Math

Match the picture to the number.
Then write how many tens and ones.

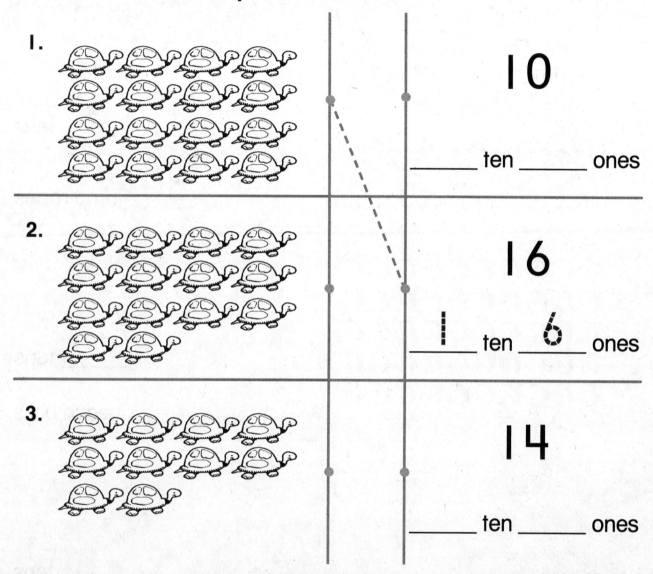

1.   1 0
                            _____ ten _____ ones

2.   1 6
                            1 ten 6 ones

3.   1 4
                            _____ ten _____ ones

 Writing and Reasoning How can you draw
to show the ones in Exercise 3?

_____

_____

Change Ones to Tens

COMMON CORE STANDARDS CC.1.NBT.2a,
CC.1.NBT.2c
Understand place value.

Circle groups of ten.
Write the numbers.

1.

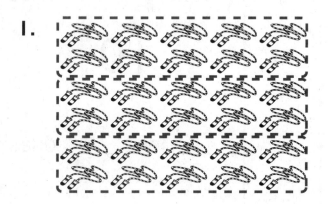

_____3_____ tens

___30___ jump ropes

2.

_____ tens

_____ beach balls

3.

_____ tens

_____ skateboards

 Writing and Reasoning If you add 30
jump ropes to Exercise 1, how many tens will you
have in all?   _____ tens

COMMON CORE STANDARD CC.1.NBT.2
Understand place value.

Ones and Tens Crossout

**Cross out the box that does not match.
Then write the missing number.**

1.

24

| 2 tens __4__ ones |
| ~~_____ tens 2 ones~~ |

2.

48

| 8 tens _____ ones |
| _____ tens 8 ones |

3.

36

| _____ tens 3 ones |
| 3 tens _____ ones |

 Writing and Reasoning How can you draw
to show that Exercise 3 is correct?

_____

_____

COMMON CORE STANDARD CC.1.NBT.2
Understand place value.

Riddles to 100

Write a number to solve.

1. I am greater than 57.

   I am less than 60.

   I have 9 ones.

   _____

2. I am greater than 72.

   I am less than 76.

   The ones are not 3 or 5.

   _____

3. I am less than 40.

   I have 8 ones and 2 tens.

   _____

4. I am less than 100.

   I have no tens. I am greater than 0 and less than 2.

   _____

5. I am greater than 35.

   I am less than 45.

   I have 2 ones.

   _____

6. I am greater than 80.

   I am less than 90.

   I have 1 one.

   _____

Writing and Reasoning Write a riddle for the number 62.

_____

_____

More Ways to Show Numbers

COMMON CORE STANDARDS CC.1.NBT.2a,
CC.1.NBT.3
Understand place value.

Match the pictures that show the same number. Write the number the pictures show.

1.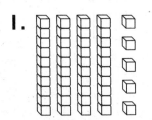

2. 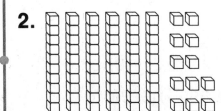 _____

3.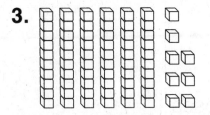

4.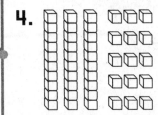

5.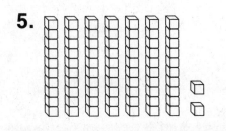

6. 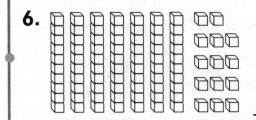 _____

7.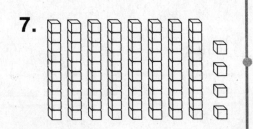

8. 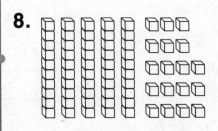 _____

 Writing and Reasoning

Draw three ways to show 47.

COMMON CORE STANDARD CC.1.NBT.1
Extend the counting sequence.

The Flower Shop

Draw quick pictures to solve.
Write the number.

> **THINK**
> Each bunch has
> 10 flowers.

1. There are 5 bunches of
   red roses. There are
   5 bunches of yellow
   roses. How many
   roses are there?

   _____ roses

2. There are 10 bunches of
   pink tulips, 5 white tulips,
   and 5 red tulips. How
   many tulips are there?

   _____ tulips

Writing and Reasoning Look at Exercise 2.
Nicole buys 3 of the red tulips and 3 of the white tulips.
Now how many tulips are there?

_____

Make a Number

COMMON CORE STANDARD CC.1.NBT.1
Extend the counting sequence

Write any digit from 0 to 9 in the blank. Then finish the drawing to match.

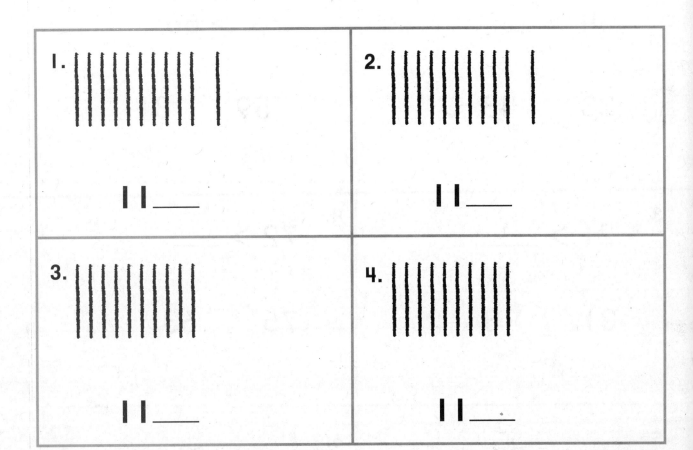

1. | | | | | | | | | | | | | | | ____

2. | | | | | | | | | | | | ____

3. | | | | | | | | | | | | ____

4. | | | | | | | | | | | | ____

 Writing and Reasoning

Finish the drawing to show 120.
Write to explain.

_____

_____

COMMON CORE STANDARD CC.1.NBT.3
Understand place value.

Which Makes It True?

Circle the number that makes
the number sentence true.

1.

34 > ___

(33)   43

2.

___ > 66

59   81

3.

21 > ___

31   13

4.

72 > ___

75   63

5.

___ > 33

34   22

6.

___ > 91

86   98

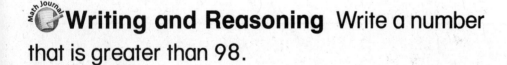

Writing and Reasoning Write a number
that is greater than 98.

_____

Which Is Less?

COMMON CORE STANDARD CC.1.NBT.3
Understand place value.

**Read the sentence. Circle true or false.
Then write the numbers to make the
comparison true.**

1. Eric said 66 is less than 51.

true

(false)

$$\underline{51} < \underline{66}$$

2. Dan said 44 is less than 46.

true

false

$$\underline{} < \underline{}$$

---

3. Anna said 81 is less
than 77.

true

false

$$\underline{} < \underline{}$$

4. Shanta said 90 is less
than 70.

true

false

$$\underline{} < \underline{}$$

---

5. Lars said 22 is less
than 33.

true

false

$$\underline{} < \underline{}$$

6. Kerry said 49 is less
than 24.

true

false

$$\underline{} < \underline{}$$

Writing and Reasoning Write four numbers
that are less than 61.

I Spy Symbols

COMMON CORE STANDARD CC.1.NBT.3
Understand place value.

**Look at the glasses. Write the numbers
and <, >, or =.**

1. (60) (64)

$$\underline{60} \; < \; \underline{64}$$

2. (77) (58)

___ ◯ ___

3. (49) (49)

___ ◯ ___

4. (81) (82)

___ ◯ ___

5. | 11 | 5 + 6 |

___ ◯ ___

6. (65) (56)

___ ◯ ___

Write numbers to make each sentence true.

7. $88 < $ ___

8. ___ $= 55$

9. ___ > 75

10. ___ > 41

Writing and Reasoning

Write your own problem.

_____

Paw Prints

Color the numbers that are less than 50 (Purple).

Color the numbers that are greater than 70 (Yellow).

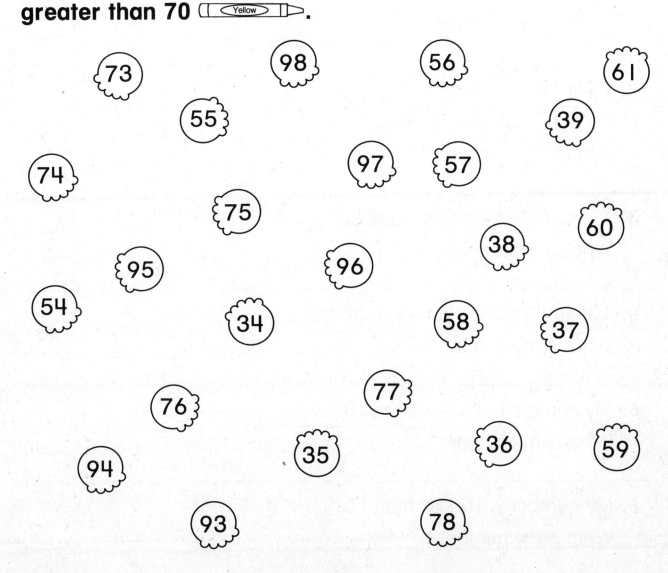

Writing and Reasoning Which numbers are both greater than 50 and less than 70?

_____

_____

What Is My Number?

COMMON CORE STANDARD CC.1.NBT.5
Use place value understanding and
properties of operations to add and subtract.

Read the riddles. Write the numbers.

1. 47 is 10 less than my number.

   67 is 10 more than my number.

   What is my number? _____

2. 75 is 10 more than my number.

   55 is 10 less than my number.

   What is my number? _____

3. 71 is 10 less than my number.

   What is my number? _____

4. 100 is 10 more than my number.

   What is my number? _____

5. My number is 10 more than 88.

   What is my number? _____

6. My number is 10 less than 10.

   What is my number? _____

 **Writing and Reasoning** Write your own riddle.

_____

_____

Good Strategy!

Write any number from 3 to 9 in the box. Choose a **strategy to help you find the sum or difference.** Then write the strategy you used. Try to use each strategy.

COMMON CORE STANDARD CC.1.OA.6
Add and subtract within 20.

Strategies I know
- count on
- count back
- doubles plus one
- doubles minus one
- make a ten
- use a related fact

1. $11 - \boxed{} = $ _____

Strategy: _____

2. $6 + \boxed{} = $ _____

Strategy: _____

3. $8 + \boxed{} = $ _____

Strategy: _____

4. $12 - \boxed{} = $ _____

Strategy: _____

5. $9 - \boxed{} = $ _____

Strategy: _____

6. $7 + \boxed{} = $ _____

Strategy: _____

 Writing and Reasoning For Exercise 4, explain why you chose the strategy you used.

_____

_____

Name _____

Treasure Tens

COMMON CORE STANDARD CC.1.NBT.4
Use place value understanding and
properties of operations to add and subtract.

Each 🔔 stands for 10. Draw the missing 🔔.
Write the missing numbers.
Then write a number sentence.

1.

___**3**___ tens + 1 ten = ___**4**___ tens

____ + ___**10**___ = ____

2.

5 tens + ____ tens = ____ tens

____ + ____ = ____

3.

4 tens + ____ tens = 6 tens

____ + ____ = ____

Writing and Reasoning Each 🔔 has
10 . Tom has 10 and 1 🔔. How many
does Tom have in all?

_____

Different Difference

COMMON CORE STANDARD CC.1.NBT.6
Use place value understanding and
properties of operations to add and subtract.

Solve. Cross out the subtraction in each row with the difference that does not match.

1. $80 - 30 = \underline{50}$ | $60 - 20 = \underline{40}$ | $70 - 20 = \underline{50}$

2. $70 - 50 = \underline{}$ | $30 - 20 = \underline{}$ | $80 - 70 = \underline{}$

3. $90 - 30 = \underline{}$ | $70 - 10 = \underline{}$ | $50 - 20 = \underline{}$

4. $60 - 40 = \underline{}$ | $90 - 80 = \underline{}$ | $50 - 40 = \underline{}$

5. $40 - 20 = \underline{}$ | $60 - 30 = \underline{}$ | $20 - 0 = \underline{}$

6. $90 - 20 = \underline{}$ | $70 - 10 = \underline{}$ | $80 - 10 = \underline{}$

7. $80 - 40 = \underline{}$ | $60 - 20 = \underline{}$ | $50 - 20 = \underline{}$

Writing and Reasoning How could you change one number in Exercise 1 to make each difference match? Explain.

_____

_____

Add Some Color

COMMON CORE STANDARD CC.1.NBT.4
Use place value understanding and
properties of operations to add and subtract.

1	2	3	4	5	6	7	8	9	10
11	12	13	14	15	16	17	18	19	20
21	22	23	24	25	26	27	28	29	30
31	32	33	34	35	36	37	38	39	40
41	42	43	44	45	46	47	48	49	50
51	52	53	54	55	56	57	58	59	60
61	62	63	64	65	66	67	68	69	70
71	72	73	74	75	76	77	78	79	80
81	82	83	84	85	86	87	88	89	90
91	92	93	94	95	96	97	98	99	100

Use the hundred chart to add. Color the sum.

1. $40 + 17 =$ _____

2. $24 + 40 =$ _____

3. $72 + 3 =$ _____

4. $42 + 4 =$ _____

5. $20 + 33 =$ _____

6. $33 + 2 =$ _____

7. $5 + 61 =$ _____

8. $14 + 30 =$ _____

Writing and Reasoning Explain two ways to use the hundred chart to find a sum of 95.

_____

_____

Tens or Ones?

COMMON CORE STANDARD CC.1.NBT.4
Use place value understanding and
properties of operations to add and subtract.

Circle the correct addend.

1. $52 + \begin{matrix} 3 \\ 30 \end{matrix} = 82$

2. $12 + \begin{matrix} 7 \\ 70 \end{matrix} = 19$

3. $44 + \begin{matrix} 4 \\ 40 \end{matrix} = 48$

4. $33 + \begin{matrix} 6 \\ 60 \end{matrix} = 39$

5. $17 + \begin{matrix} 2 \\ 20 \end{matrix} = 37$

6. $11 + \begin{matrix} 8 \\ 80 \end{matrix} = 91$

 Writing and Reasoning In Exercise 1, how did you decide which addend was correct?

_____

_____

_____

Berry Easy Addition

COMMON CORE STANDARD CC.1.NBT.4
Use place value understanding and
properties of operations to add and subtract.

Add. Circle the strawberries that have the same sum.

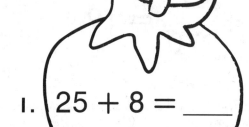

1. $25 + 8 =$ ___

2. $30 + 6 =$ ___

3. $27 + 9 =$ ___

4. $29 + 7 =$ ___

5. $31 + 4 =$ ___

Writing and Reasoning Explain how you could make the other strawberries match the sum.

_____

_____

Add and Match

COMMON CORE STANDARD CC.1.NBT.4
Use place value understanding and
properties of operations to add and subtract.

**Match the addition with its sum. Then match
tens or ones to make the number.**

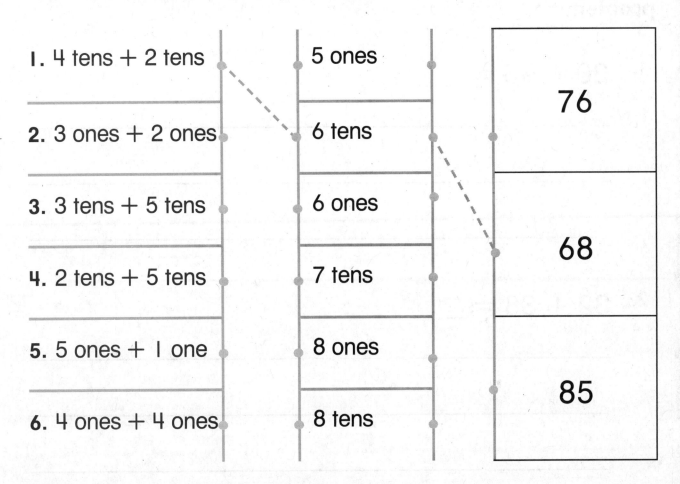

1. 4 tens + 2 tens
2. 3 ones + 2 ones
3. 3 tens + 5 tens
4. 2 tens + 5 tens
5. 5 ones + 1 one
6. 4 ones + 4 ones

5 ones
6 tens
6 ones
7 tens
8 ones
8 tens

76
68
85

 Writing and Reasoning How did you
match Exercise 3?

_____

_____

_____

What Is the Problem?

COMMON CORE STANDARD CC.1.NBT.4
Use place value understanding and
properties of operations to add and subtract.

**Use each addition sentence to write your
own word problem. Then solve your word
problem.**

1. $20 + 43 =$ ___

_____

_____

_____

2. $32 + 38 =$ ___

_____

_____

_____

Writing and Reasoning Choose one of the
problems. Explain how you solved it.

_____

_____

_____

Use the Clue

COMMON CORE STANDARDS CC. 1.NBT.4,
CC.1.NBT.6
Use place value understanding and properties of
operations to add and subtract.

**Use the clue to write the number
you add or subtract. Then solve.**

1. The second number is 10 less than the first number.	$38 - \underline{\quad} = \underline{\quad}$
2. The second number has 5 more ones than the first number.	$22 + \underline{\quad} = \underline{\quad}$
3. The second number has 3 tens and 4 ones.	$9 + \underline{\quad} = \underline{\quad}$
4. The second number has 0 tens and 0 ones.	$55 + \underline{\quad} = \underline{\quad}$

Writing and Reasoning Write a clue for an addend
in the number sentence $15 + 25 = 40$.

_____

_____

COMMON CORE STANDARD CC.1.MD.1
Measure lengths indirectly and by iterating length units.

Shortest and Longest

Order by length. Write 1, 2, or 3.

1. Order from **shortest** to **longest**.

1
3
2

2. Order from **longest** to **shortest**.

_____
_____
_____

3. Order from **longest** to **shortest**.

_____
_____
_____

4. Order from **shortest** to **longest**.

_____
_____
_____

Writing and Reasoning Draw three objects in order from **longest** to **shortest**.

Pencil Comparisons

Draw the lengths of the objects.

1. The pencil is shorter than the marker.

   The marker is shorter than the drinking straw.

   The drinking straw and the string are the same length.

pencil	
marker	
straw	
string	

2. The pencil is longer than the yarn.

   The yarn is longer than the crayon.

   The yarn and the ribbon are the same length.

pencil	
yarn	
ribbon	
crayon	

Writing and Reasoning Is the pencil shortest in Exercise 1 and longest in Exercise 2? Explain.

_____

_____

_____

Tile Measure

COMMON CORE STANDARD CC.1.MD.2
Measure lengths indirectly and by iterating length units.

Read the problem.
Use 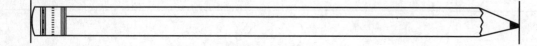 **to measure.**

1. This ribbon belongs to Janet.
About how many ■ long is it?

about _____ ■

2. This rope belongs to Ron.
About how many ■ long is it?

about _____ ■

3. This marker belongs to Erica.
About how many ■ long is it?

about _____ ■

Writing and Reasoning Miguel has a
pencil that is about 8 ■ long. Is the pencil below
longer, shorter, or about the same length as
Miguel's pencil? _____

Compare Measurements

COMMON CORE STANDARD CC.1.MD.2
Measure lengths indirectly and by iterating length units.

Use the measuring tool you made to compare. Circle which is longer.

1. Measure your finger and a book.

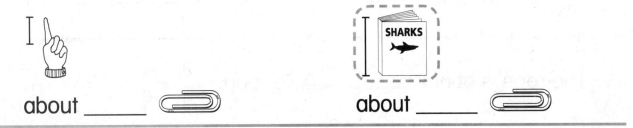

about _____ 　　　　about _____

2. Measure your shoe and an eraser.

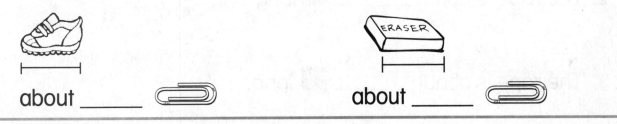

about _____ 　　　　about _____

3. Measure a crayon and your book bag.

about _____ 　　　　about _____

Writing and Reasoning How could you find the measurement around your wrist? Explain.

_____

_____

_____

Measuring Units

COMMON CORE STANDARD CC.1.MD.2
Measure lengths indirectly and by iterating
length units.

**Measure the rope. Use different units
of measure.**

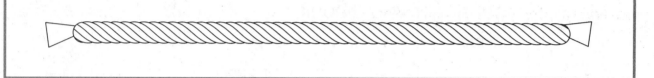

1. The rope is about _____ 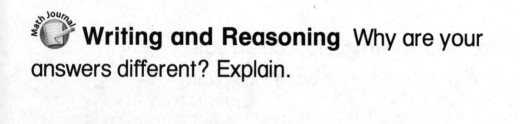 long.

2. The rope is about _____ ▪ long.

3. The rope is about _____ ▪ long.

4. The rope is about _____ _____ long.

5. The rope is about _____ _____ long.

Writing and Reasoning Why are your
answers different? Explain.

_____

_____

_____

_____

Name _____

COMMON CORE STANDARD CC.1.MD.3
Tell and write time.

Mixed Up Clocks

Write each time.
Write 1, 2, or 3 to show the times in order.

1.

☐

2.

3   ☐   ☐

Writing and Reasoning How can you look at
a clock and know what time it will be one hour later?

_____

_____

_____

COMMON CORE STANDARD CC.1.MD.3
Tell and write time.

Time Patterns

Look for the pattern in each row.
Circle the clock that comes next.

Writing and Reasoning When it is half past 5:00, is the hour hand closer to the 5 or the 6? Explain.

_____

A Time Path

COMMON CORE STANDARD CC.1.MD.3
Tell and write time.

Start at 9:00. Connect to show the times every half hour. Write the time that does not belong.

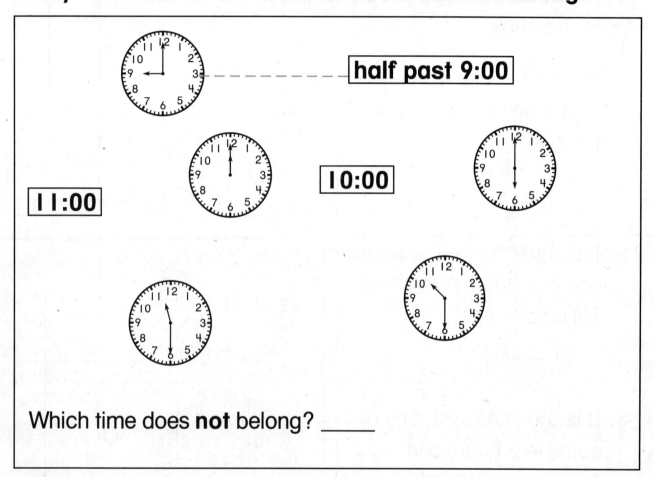

half past 9:00

10:00

11:00

Which time does **not** belong? _____

Writing and Reasoning Where does the minute hand always point when it is half past the hour? Explain.

_____

_____

_____

COMMON CORE STANDARD CC.1.MD.3
Tell and write time.

Time for Play

Jake and his friends are ready to play.
Draw hands on each clock to show the time.
Write the time.

1. It is 3:00. Jake will play ball in 30 minutes. What time will it be?

_____

2. It is 4:00. Mei will walk her dog in 2 hours. What time will it be?

_____

3. It is 5:00. Asa will play a game in 2 hours and 30 minutes. What time will it be?

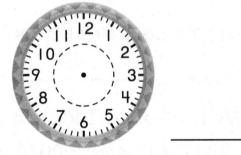

_____

Writing and Reasoning Explain how you solved Exercise 2.

_____

_____

_____

COMMON CORE STANDARD CC.1.MD.4
Represent and interpret data.

A Pair of Picture Graphs

Blake made this picture graph.

Season We Like					
☀ summer	♟	♟	♟	♟	♟
⛄ winter	♟	♟	♟		

Each ♟ stands for 1 child.

Divya made this picture graph.

Pet We Like				
🐟 fish	○	○		
🐦 bird	○	○	○	○

Each ○ stands for 1 child.

Write a question about each picture graph.
Show the answer.

1. _____

_____

_____

2. _____

_____

_____

 Writing and Reasoning How are the
two graphs alike? How are they different?

_____

_____

_____

COMMON CORE STANDARD CC.1.MD.4
Represent and interpret data.

Party Time Picture Graph

**Follow the directions to complete
the picture graph.**

1. Jill has 5 🎩 .
   She has 3 more 🎈 than 🎩 .
   She has 2 more 🎁 than 🎩 .

Jill's Party Supplies									
🎩 hats									
🎈 balloons									
🎁 bags									

Each ○ stands for 1 item.

There will be 8 children at Jill's party.

Use the picture graph to answer each question.

2. Does Jill have a 🎈 for
   each child? Circle.

   yes   no

3. Each child gets one 🎩 .
   How many more 🎩 does
   Jill need?

   _____ more 🎩

Writing and Reasoning Jill gets 1 more .
Will she have a bag for each child? Explain.

_____

_____

Name _____

COMMON CORE STANDARD CC.1.MD.4
Represent and interpret data.

Bar Graph Clues

Use the bar graph to complete each sentence.

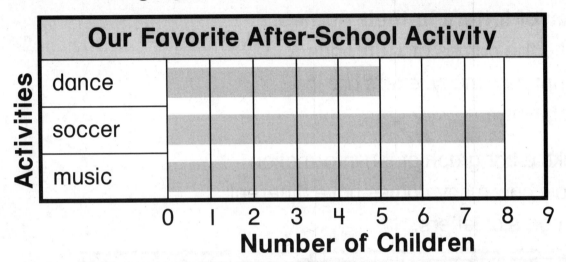

1. _____ more children chose soccer than dance.

_____

2. _____ fewer children chose music than soccer.

_____

3. _____ children chose dance or music.

_____

4. If 3 more children chose dance, then the bar graph
   would show _____ children for dance.

Writing and Reasoning How can you tell
without counting if more children chose soccer than
music? Explain.

_____

_____

COMMON CORE STANDARD CC.1.MD.4
Represent and interpret data.

Compare the Letters

**Some children are comparing the
number of letters in their names.**

1. Write the names of 10 friends.
   Count how many letters are in
   each name.

2. Make a bar graph of the information.
   Show how many names have different
   numbers of letters.

The Number of Letters in Our Name										
7 or more										
6 letters										
5 letters										
4 letters										
3 letters										
2 letters										

Number of Letters (vertical axis label)

0 1 2 3 4 5 6 7 8 9 10

Number of Children

3. How many letters are in the most names? _____

Writing and Reasoning How would the
graph change if you added your name? Explain.

_____

Trip Tally

COMMON CORE STANDARD CC.1.MD.4
Represent and interpret data.

Complete the tally chart.

Our Favorite Trip		Total
🐘 zoo	II	
🐃 museum	⊬⊬⊬ ⊬⊬⊬ I	
📖 library	⊬⊬⊬ II	

Use the tally chart to solve.

1. Jen is one of 11 children who chose this trip. Which trip is it?

_____

2. 5 more children chose this trip than the zoo trip. Which trip is it?

_____

3. The fewest number of children chose this trip. Which trip is it?

_____

Writing and Reasoning Write another clue that can be answered by using the chart. Then solve.

_____

_____

Color Count

COMMON CORE STANDARD CC.1.MD.4
Represent and interpret data.

Color some circles red.

Color some blue.

Color some yellow.

Make a tally chart to show how many of each color.

Circles I Colored		Total
red		
blue		
yellow		

Use your tally chart to answer each question.

1. How many circles did you color red or blue?

   _____ circles

2. Did you color more blue circles or yellow circles?

   _____ circles

3. Did you color fewer yellow circles or red circles?

   _____ circles

Writing and Reasoning How does the tally chart help you count and compare the colored circles?

_____

_____

Favorite Seasons

COMMON CORE STANDARD CC.1.MD.4
Represent and interpret data.

Find out about your friends' favorite seasons.

1. Write a question you can ask 10 friends.

_____

2. Ask 10 friends. Use the information to make a bar graph.

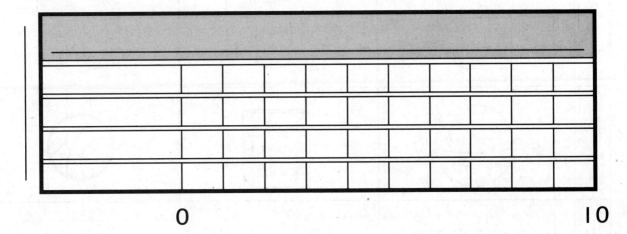

0   10

_____

3. Which season was chosen most often? _____

4. Which season was chosen the least? _____

Writing and Reasoning Write another question that can be answered by your graph.

_____

_____

Match the Shapes

COMMON CORE STANDARD CC.1.G.1
Reason with shapes and their attributes.

Draw lines to connect the
three shapes that match.

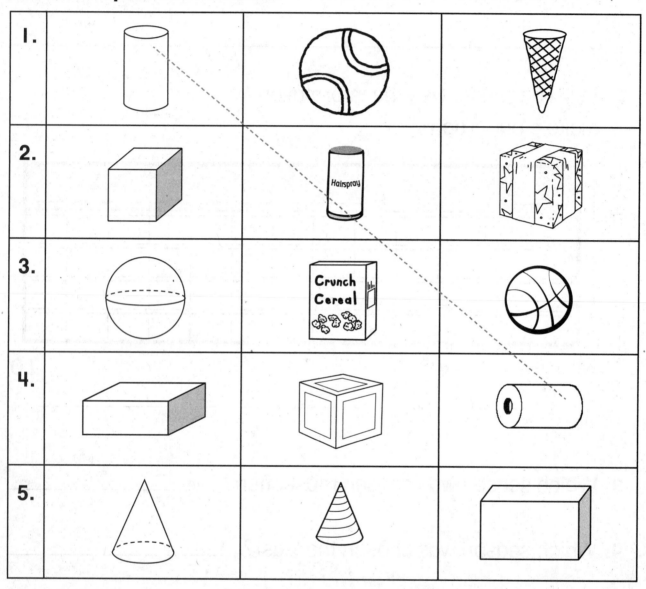

Writing and Reasoning Circle each shape
that has two or more flat surfaces.

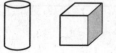

What's New?

COMMON CORE STANDARD CC.1.G.2
Reason with shapes and their attributes.

Three children made new shapes. Circle the shape that matches the description.

1. Jill's shape has a cube on the bottom and a cylinder on the top.

2. Roberto's shape has two rectangular prisms.

 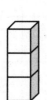

3. Lin's shape has a cylinder and a cone.

 Writing and Reasoning Think of a shape you want to make. Write a description for it.

_____

_____

Make New Shapes

COMMON CORE STANDARD CC.1.G.2
Reason with shapes and their attributes.

Here is a shape.
Repeat and combine.
Which new shapes can you make?
Circle the correct shapes.
Cross out the wrong shapes.

1.	**2.**	**3.**
4.	**5.**	**6.**
7.	**8.**	**9.**

Writing and Reasoning How were you able to make different shapes?

_____

COMMON CORE STANDARD CC.1.G.2
Reason with shapes and their attributes.

Shape Structures

Max is building objects. Circle the shapes he will need for each object.

1.

post

2.

steps

3.

shelf

4.

top

Writing and Reasoning Is there another answer for Exercise 2? Explain.

_____

_____

Shapes in Objects

COMMON CORE STANDARD CC.1.G.1
Reason with shapes and their attributes.

Color the flat surfaces each object has.

1.	(cube)	△ ☐ ◯ ▭
2.	(SOUP can)	△ ☐ ◯ ▭
3.	(gift box)	△ ☐ ◯ ▭
4.	(book)	△ ☐ ◯ ▭

Writing and Reasoning Find a three-dimensional object. Draw the object and a flat surface of the object.

COMMON CORE STANDARD CC.1.G.1
Reason with shapes and their attributes.

Shape Groups

Cross out the shapes that do not belong.

1.	We have 4 vertices. We have 4 sides. All of our sides are the same length.	△ □ ○ ▭ ◇
2.	We have more than 2 sides. We do not have 4 sides.	▢ △ ◇ ▭ ▽

Draw a shape to solve.

3.	I have 3 vertices. I have 3 sides.	
4.	I have 4 sides. I have 4 vertices. My sides are not all the same length.	

Writing and Reasoning Draw two different shapes that have 4 vertices and 4 sides.

COMMON CORE STANDARD CC.1.G.1
Reason with shapes and their attributes.

Riddle Shapes

Circle the shape that answers the riddle.

1.	I have more than 4 vertices. I have more than 5 sides. Which shape am I?	
2.	I have 4 sides. I have 4 vertices. My sides are not all the same length.	

3. Sort ▢, △, ⬡, ⬠, and ▱ into two groups. Draw to show your work.

3 or 4 vertices	more than 4 vertices

Writing and Reasoning Draw a shape that has 5 vertices and 5 sides.

Shape Maker

COMMON CORE STANDARD CC.1.G.2
Reason with shapes and their attributes.

**Use pattern blocks. Draw lines to show how
to make each shape.**

1. Use ⬡.

2. Use △.

3. Use △.

4. Use △.

 Writing and Reasoning Draw lines to show

how this ⬡ can be made from 3 △ and 1 ▱.

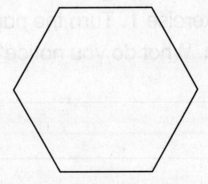

Shapes and More Shapes

COMMON CORE STANDARD CC.1.G.2
Reason with shapes and their attributes.

You can color to combine shapes.

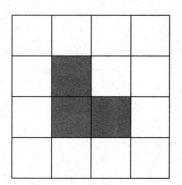 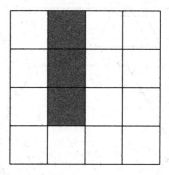

1. Color 4 ☐ to make a combined shape.
   Make as many different shapes as you can.

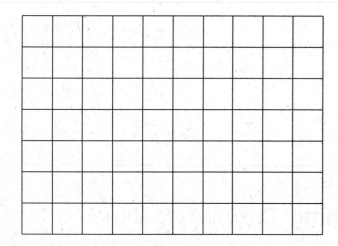

Writing and Reasoning Look at the shapes you drew in Exercise 1. Turn the paper to see them upside down. What do you notice?

_____

_____

Name _____

Shapes in a Shape

COMMON CORE STANDARDS CC.1.G.2
Reason with shapes and their attributes.

Use △. Show how the △ makes the ◇.
Draw lines. Then show how the ◇ makes
the ⬡. Draw lines.

1. Use 2 △.

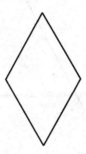 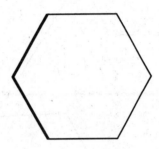

---

2. Use 3 △.

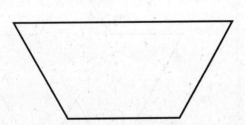 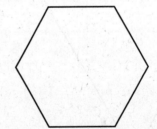

Writing and Reasoning How many △
do you need to make 2 ⬡?

_____ △

Build a Shape

Put three pattern blocks together
to make each shape.
Draw to show your model.

COMMON CORE STANDARD CC.1.G.2
Reason with shapes and their attributes.

1.

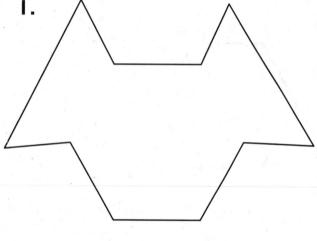

2.

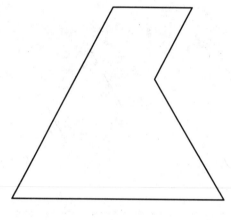

3.

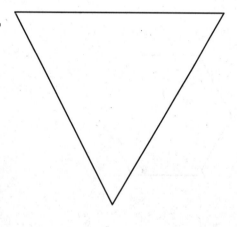

4.

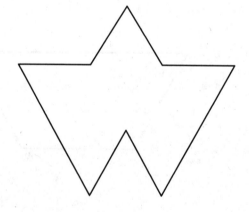

 Writing and Reasoning On a separate
sheet of paper, draw a different shape using 3 of
the shapes above.

How Many Triangles?

COMMON CORE STANDARD CC.1.G.2
Reason with shapes and their attributes.

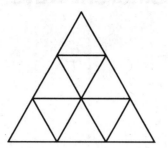

Use the picture above. Find as many triangles as you can. Write how many.

1. _____

2. _____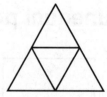

3. _____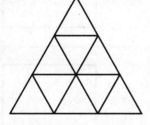

4. _____ triangles in all

 Writing and Reasoning How did you find the triangles in Exercise 2? Explain.

_____

_____

_____

Four Parts, Four Ways

COMMON CORE STANDARD CC.1.G.3
Reason with shapes and their attributes.

Show 4 equal parts 4 different ways.

1.

2.

3.

4.

Show 4 unequal parts 4 different ways.

5.

6.

7.

8.

 **Writing and Reasoning** Is a part from Exercise 1 the same size as a part from Exercise 2? Explain.

_____

_____

_____

COMMON CORE STANDARD CC.1.G.3
Reason with shapes and their attributes.

Missing Halves

**The picture shows half of the whole.
Draw the other half.**

1.

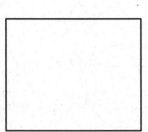

2.

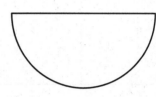

3.

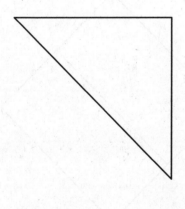

4.

 Writing and Reasoning Do any of your whole shapes match? Explain.

_____

_____

_____

From Halves to Fourths

COMMON CORE STANDARD CC.1.G.3
Reason with shapes and their attributes.

These shapes show halves.
Draw lines to make them show fourths.

1.

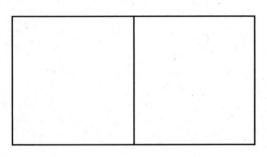

2.

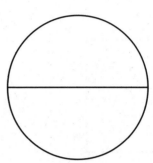

3.

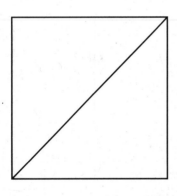

4.

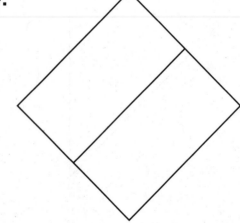

Writing and Reasoning Tell how you can solve Exercise 1 in a different way.

_____

_____